LIVE THE LIFE YOU HAVE IMAGINED!

Simple Ways to Begin Living Your Best Life

Janie Jurkovich

It's never too late to start living your best life!
Janie J

Live The Life You Have Imagined! Simple Ways to Begin Living Your Best Life

By Janie Jurkovich

Copyright © 2018

Golden Spiral Press ™ is a trademark of Janie Jurkovich

Book Design and Editing by Beth Bridges, eBridge Marketing

Cover Design by Ellie Dote, Ellie Girl Creations

Author Photo by Suzanne Moles, Wattleweb Global Solutions

First Edition: June 2018
Published by Golden Spiral Press
Fresno, California
www.JanieJ.net

"If one advances confidently in the direction of her dreams, and endeavors to live the life which she has imagined, she will meet with success unexpected in common hours."

Henry David Thoreau

DEDICATION

This book is dedicated to all the women who, by their actions, small and large, have encouraged me and other women to transform their lives from merely existing to taking positive steps to live their best life.

For those women who have not yet begun to live the life of their dreams, there is no time like the present to begin. Just say "NO" to the naysayers and move your life ahead, one step at a time.

Here's to all of you who choose to start the journey and live the life you have imagined!

ACKNOWLEDGEMENT

I would be remiss to not acknowledge that the fire within me to publish this book was fanned by the ridicule from my former husband. He did not understand that some women actually desire to improve their lives.

CONTENTS

A LIFE YOU ONLY IMAGINED

A butterfly emerges from her cocoon.

She's wary to venture out into the world,
but excited at the same time.

She thinks, "Will I make it ?
What's in store for me in this big, pretentious world?"

As she fervently flaps her wings, she discovers the world to be
a beautiful, wondrous place full of adventure.

The sunlit trees beckon her. The flowers shimmer in the wind.

She becomes immersed in living a life
she could have only imagined.

We are the butterflies in our own life.

Break free; meet the challenges and reap the rewards of a life
you only imagined.

~ Janie Jurkovich

INTRODUCTION

his short book is derived from my own struggles, later in life, once my children and spouse were gone and I realized my life was totally out of control.

I realized I had not spent the time required to build my own life. I sought to figure out the basics of what would lead me to the life I once imagined. I used these steps to get a handle on my own life and continue to improve it.

Originally, this book was a weekly blog post in an attempt to shed some light on what we as women can do to live our best life. It was written for those women (30-70 years old) already experiencing a busy family and work life but striving to put some joy and balance back into it.

How to Use This Book

The purpose of the book is to start with the basics, simple ways to get better, a little at a time, so women can work towards developing a better life. This is not a quick "fix it" book where you read it once, suddenly absorb everything and then live a perfect life.

Instead, the book is a stepping off point where one assimilates the steps into her everyday life and develops and grows into the life she imagines for herself.

To fully learn from this book, it must be slowly digested, read, and re-read until it becomes part of one's everyday life.

We can all do these steps on our own, but only the most vigilant can benefit from the self-direction and introspection required. A suggested alternative is to read, digest and discuss this book with a group of like-minded ladies.

Perhaps your female networking friends, business associates, or other women's group, would find such discussions helpful. Find or create your own group and encourage each other to "Live the Life You Have Imagined."

Supplemental questions to help guide your discussions are included at the end of each chapter. Write your thoughts and answers directly in this book.

Or, if you'd like more room to write, you can download all the questions in one single, printable document — a free gift - by going to www.JanieJ.net/bonus.

Once you've finished reading this book and you've put it on the shelf, make an appointment on your calendar for six months from now to revisit your answers and compare your life then to now.

You'll be amazed and inspired by how far you've come.

CHAPTER ONE

LIVE THE LIFE
YOU HAVE IMAGINED

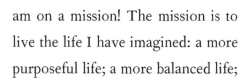 am on a mission! The mission is to
live the life I have imagined: a more
purposeful life; a more balanced life;
a life with time spent with family and friends; a life with time spent
doing things I enjoy like traveling and tending to my small farm;
and a life with less worry.

The life you imagine will be specific to you, but some of the
tactics will be the same. Join me on my journey as I share the
lessons I have learned and how I am consciously working towards
living the life I imagined.

JANIE JURKOVICH

CHAPTER TWO

THE FIRST STEP

 et's begin with the first step of evaluating your life. Decide what you really want, not what your parents, spouse or Aunt Sally, think your life should be. Take inventory of where you are presently and where you want to be in order to live the life you have imagined.

One way to determine this is to write a list of how you spend your day now. Then write another list of how you would like to spend your day. Think about each item and what it would really take to make it happen.

You need to look at the long-term also. Even if your daily life is great, is it getting you where you want to be in the future? Nothing is impossible, but you have to take that first step and get going in the right direction.

Without evaluating your situation and deciding where to go, it is a certainty that you won't get there!

Set some goals and start in that direction. Don't worry about how long it will take. Deciding what you want and making changes to get there is most of the battle. The rest is repetition and following a plan.

Goals are seldom met unless they are accompanied by a plan, so next make a plan to get there. What steps would be necessary to make those changes? Write them all down. Organize them in the proper order.

Think of it as a draft plan, because you will modify and improve it along the way. But at least you will be moving forward. It is much easier to course correct while moving.

We spend most of our time just trying to get started, so take that first step!

Chapter Two
Discussion Questions

1. How did your two lists of your daily life NOW versus what you would LIKE compare? Were they fairly close or way off?
2. What did this exercise teach you about how you are living now? Is it all off-the cuff emergencies or is it purposeful?
3. What adjustments can you make to your current life easily and start incorporating into your daily routine?
4. What long-term goal or goals did you set? Are they stretch-goals, or easier, more attainable ones?
5. Give an example of the steps to achieve one of your goals.

My Goals:

(Not enough room to write? Get a free downloadable copy of all the questions at www.JanieJ.net/bonus)

JANIE JURKOVICH

CHAPTER THREE

SLEEP

 leep 7 to 8 hours a night. It's amazing what we can accomplish when we are properly rested! The "foggy brain" disappears, decisions are easier to make, and you have enough energy to make it through the day.

Everyone's body is different. Some people can get by with only 6 hours of sleep (so I have heard), but most of us need 7-8 hours per night. Sleep is not a luxury – it is a medical necessity.

Try going to bed at a set time each night and your body will automatically wake up when it is rested. Prepare mentally for sleep.

Turn off the technology and have a quiet routine like listening to relaxing music, a hot bath, meditation or reading a real book. (No reading via technology because the light stimulates our brain.)

I have tried doing this and found I am an eight hour-a-night gal. It's almost like clockwork. If I short-change myself, I feel it all day long. Multiple days in a row and I am really tired.

If you aren't sure how much sleep you need, try this: keep a log of hours slept and then write down how you felt during the day.

Did you have enough energy? Was your mind clear and able to focus? How did you feel at the end of the day – exhausted or accomplished? These are all clues as to whether you are getting enough sleep.

Make sleep a priority!

Chapter Three
Discussion Questions

1. How did you determine the right amount of sleep for you?
2. What happens if you DON'T get enough sleep? What happens when you DO get enough sleep?
3. Do you notice any changes in your levels of competency and/or attitude when you lack sufficient sleep?
4. What can you do to ensure you get enough sleep? Any tips to share?

My Plan For Proper Sleep:

JANIE JURKOVICH

EAT HEALTHY

o many choices. So many unhealthy temptations. So little time. It seems difficult to eat healthy when you are busy. It is much easier to go on autopilot and eat take-out or stop at a fast food restaurant.

The best way to counter-act this madness is to plan ahead. Even with the best of intentions, a hungry stomach will opt for the quick fix anytime. Take your lunch, snacks and water with you when possible. Plan your evening meals before you shop for the week.

Consciously think about which restaurant to meet your friends/business associates for lunch. Select a location with suitable menu choices.

If you do eat out, make good (healthy) choices. Check calories and content. I remember taking my children to a pizza place for lunch and getting my usual salad while they had pizza. Then I noticed the salad dressing had nearly the same calories as the pizza.

What an eye opener! If you are going to splurge, make sure it is worth it to you.

A good place to start your meal planning is with a balanced diet. Your doctor or a nutritionist can help you or at least point you in the right direction.

It is a smart idea to plan your meals, even if it is loosely planning your meals for most nights during the week. When you do the shopping and food preparations, you can control the calories, the sugar, the fat and the carbs. If you have special dietary needs this is all the more important.

Cooking at home is not really all that daunting, it is mostly in the preparation. If you have the basics at home and shop regularly it can save you a lot of time and money.

It doesn't have to be a time-consuming task either. Food can be semi-prepared ahead of time. You can buy prepared segments of the meal to cut down on food preparation.

Just keep it simple with fresh fruits, vegetables and lean protein. One trick is to prepare your veggies once a week by cleaning, slicing and packaging them for quicker cooking during the week.

Another tip is to cook your meat, chicken or fish on the weekend then use the leftovers for a couple of quick meals during the week.

Change up the rest of the meal so it doesn't seem like you are eating leftovers. As an example: roast chicken on day 1; chicken tacos on day 2; and chicken soup on day 3 (if it lasts that long). Another trick to avoid boring meals is to add nuts, raisins, and different spices.

Preparing your evening meal can be a fun way to connect with family members or friends. You can share kitchen tasks and spend time together. Even cooking solo has the benefit of unwinding at the end of the day.

If you don't think healthy meal planning is worth the effort, consider how much you spend eating out in a month. Compare that to buying and preparing healthy, good-tasting meals suited to your taste at home and you will discover an incentive to save all that money. Your body will thank you!

Chapter Four
Discussion Questions

1. What one action could you take to improve your eating habits?
2. Give some examples of changes you have made to improve your eating habits.
3. Share some of your meal preparation tips with the group.
4. What steps have you taken to enlist the help of others with meal preparation?
5. Figure out how much you spend on eating out each month versus buying groceries. Think about what you could spend that money on instead.
6. What healthy options have you found at the grocery store or restaurants?

My Eating Plan:

JANIE JURKOVICH

CHAPTER FIVE
EXERCISE

We all know we should exercise, but that doesn't necessarily give us enough incentive to actually put on the sneakers and go for a walk.

How about your chances of living longer? How about reducing your health risks? How about being around to see your grandkids?

These are all excellent reasons to exercise!

The other biggie is that it makes you feel better. Your mind is clearer and your mood improves when you exercise.

Just think how good you will feel!

For best results pick something you actually enjoy. It will be easier to stick with it! It could be golfing, swimming, gardening, cycling, walking the dog or whatever you like to do on a regular basis.

Perhaps your routine needs to be updated so it doesn't get boring. That works for some folks too. Try new activities until you find something you enjoy.

If you are feeling too out of shape to start, just start! Do something, even if it is just a walk around the block. Eventually you can make two blocks, ¼ mile, ½ mile, and so on. You might even consider a slow jog at a later date.

The hardest part is just deciding to start. Then the "habit" needs to kick in so it becomes part of your lifestyle. That's why you need to find an activity you enjoy.

Maybe you are one of those ladies who needs a group activity so you have accountability if you don't show up. Or perhaps you are the type that needs to have some money on the table to make you follow through.

If you pre-paid for your pilates class, are you more likely to participate?

Think about your thought process and outsmart yourself so you will be successful! Once you decide you are going to do some sort of exercise on a specific day, the question is WHAT activity am I going to do, not when, if or maybe.

Your eventual goal is to have an automatic habit to exercise.

Chapter Five
Discussion Questions

1. What is your motivation for exercising?
2. What type of activities do you prefer? Do you like group or individual activities?
3. How can you make exercise a regular part of your life?
4. When do you plan to exercise – morning, afternoon, evening or other?

My Exercise Plan:

CHAPTER SIX

MEDITATE

his doesn't necessarily mean breathing and repeating "om," although it could. It just refers to a quiet time set aside, preferably daily, to relax and help you in a way that is incomprehensible to those of us super-busy folks, until you actually try it.

For some people, meditating means reflecting on the many things in your life for which you are grateful.

For others it can mean sitting quietly and just thinking, praying, or asking for guidance from your spiritual leader.

If you want to hear God, you need to listen, and you can't listen if you are always busy doing and thinking.

The quietness helps put your life back in perspective. Just relaxing and letting your mind wander can also make use of your intuitive mind. Answers to questions may come to you in the space between your thoughts, if you are quiet and still long enough. Meditating improves your mood and calms you.

It can help you find answers and peace within yourself. I prefer to do it in the morning, but others enjoy a little retreat mid-day or in the evening. Regular meditation will help you reach a relaxed state more quickly.

I must say, meditating or quiet time has been a true life-changing practice for me. In times of difficulty or stress, it was just what I needed to come out of the gloom.

It helps with self-reflection, problem solving, mood lifting, and getting my day off to a great start.

Chapter Six
Discussion Questions

1. Do you practice meditation or quiet time regularly? If so, what is your style of meditating? (There is no right answer.) Are you aware there are many types of mediation from different cultures and religions?

2. Where do you or could you easily and comfortably practice meditation?

3. When is a good time for you to meditate?

4. What changes could you make to fit in a little time for yourself to meditate?

5. What benefits have you gained from meditating?

My Meditation Plan:

JANIE JURKOVICH

READ DAILY

Reading is great for your mind and soul! It is important to set aside a specific amount of time each day for reading – even 15 minutes, and guard it carefully. Typically, I read early in the morning. It gets the day off to a good start, one with a positive outlook and relaxed manner.

Perhaps bedtime reading, during your lunch or for an afternoon break suits you better. Find what works with you and your schedule.

Read all types of books – from personal development to ancient civilizations, or biographies, and spiritual books. There is something to be learned from them all!

Note: work/professional articles and Facebook do not count! You will be reading those anyway. The purpose is to read something new.

Well-known personal motivator, Zig Ziglar, was known to read for hours each day. No wonder he was so insightful!

Reading opens your mind to new ideas. You start to see things from a new perspective. This is helpful not just with work (like during contract negotiations), but in personal relationships. It makes you think – "how does my spouse, friend, or co-worker feel about X."

When you're reading, concentrate on the topic. It provides a great escape.

Chapter Seven
Discussion Questions

1. How and when were you able to set aside reading time?
2. Give an example of some of the books or articles you have read.
3. What topic have you read about that sparked an interest for future exploration?
4. Have any articles or books changed your mind or offered insights?

My Reading Plan:

JANIE JURKOVICH

SAY "NO" TO THE SHOULDS

*W*e all have a lot of "stuff" to do, it seems. I should attend this event. I should volunteer there. I should clean out the pantry. These "shoulds" fill our heads with clutter and guilt while distracting us from the real meaning in our lives.

Before we know it, we are on overload! We are tired and

cranky and not doing any of the things we want to do! Our life is busy, but not fulfilling or in some cases, even happy.

Do we really have to do it all?

Stop and spend a moment to think about each item. Is it really necessary? What would happen if you declined? Are the consequences really that dire?

Don't feel compelled to offer an explanation. Remember, it is YOUR life and your choices are not for someone else to judge.

Some good advice – if it doesn't add value to your life and move you forward on your goals, just say "No, thank you."

Chapter Eight
Discussion Questions

1. What activities could you say "No" to?

2. How much time do you spend each week doing "No" items?

3. What could you have done with that time if you had the courage to say "No"?

4. After answering these questions, do you think you could move more items to the "No" side?

My Plan for Saying "No:" *(Write some suggested scripts)*

STRIVE FOR WORK/LIFE HARMONY, NOT BALANCE

he word "balance" conjures up a vision of equality such as the judicial scale.

Work and life balance is a challenge for nearly everyone.

It's a virtual impossibility and a phrase that leads to guilt and unhappiness because we are unable to attain it. If we strive for "harmony," there is more of a sense of give and take, according to the needs of the moment.

At times we need to take care of a sick child or elderly parents or some other "life" or family emergency. Knowing your top priority in each area and focusing on that task when you need to will help immensely.

You may even be able to incorporate your work/life activities. For example, if your top "work" priority is reading a report, bring it with you while you are tending to a sick child. You can ease back into "work" as soon as your "life" priority allows.

The key is moving seamlessly back and forth between the two, while keep up with your top priorities. Spending a few minutes alone to meditate or calm yourself may make all the difference in tackling your newest challenge. Take a deep breath and step into it.

Remind yourself that things don't always go as planned and learn to go with the flow, making adjustments as you can. Learning how to adapt to life's constant changes and challenges is something we all need to do.

It takes time and conscious effort.

Chapter Nine
Discussion Questions

1. What work/life challenges have you encountered?

2. How have you handled them?

3. Do you ever feel guilty or incompetent? (Recognize when this happens and resolve not to let it guide you to do things you do not really have to do.)

4. How would a different perspective help you see such challenges in a new light?

My Plan to Deal with Work/Life Harmony: (*List priorities or scenarios that might help you focus on this skill*)

SCHEDULE DOWNTIME

ne way to enjoy yourself a little more on this journey through life, is to schedule downtime.

Regular one or two-week vacations from work do more than soothe our souls and help us rest. They actually help us to improve our functioning at work when we return to the job.

When we know we have a vacation scheduled, most of us will typically work harder than usual to get things in order before we leave.

We seem to see the end (or prize) in sight, so we are willing to push a little harder.

But if you wait until you have the time, funds or inclination, it may not happen. The best laid plans are those you actually PLAN! That means sitting down and planning out your vacations (yep, I said *vacations*) at the beginning of the year.

Pencil them in on your calendar. A beach trip, a camping trip, time in the mountains, or a visit with relatives in another state. Whatever you want to do. Set reminders on your calendar a few months ahead to actually tend to the details. It's best to set up a budget and a way to save for those vacations too.

It WILL all come together with a little planning! Don't fall victim to the thought, "I can't afford it." It is simply not true. You could save money for a European vacation if you planned it and saved a little money each week by cutting out unnecessary expenses.

You can do it if you really want to!

Short "fun" activities can really help you make it through the week, too. A night out with friends, even if it is a networking dinner, will be a welcomed change of pace compared to pouring over financial documents or reviewing reports (for those with workaholic tendencies) or vegging out at home (for those more laid-back folks).

I have found if I don't plan it, put it on my schedule, and pay for it, it won't happen. There always seems to be an excuse not to participate in these "extra" activities when the time comes. But if it is on the schedule, then it happens.

Once I attend, my mood is lifted, I am energized, and I have a great time. I am never sorry that I pushed myself to attend.

Downtime, like sleep, is a necessity! It is part of taking care of yourself. No one else is going to do it for you, unless it is your travel agent. And even with her, you have to give her a time-line and budget. Let there be no excuses! This is a great way to live a wonderful life.

As a side note, for many years we did not go on vacations due to the usual excuses, no time off work, no money, and too difficult to coordinate schedules. Once I decided that enough was enough, I found a way to make 4 trips to Europe in 5 years without declaring bankruptcy.

There were family and friends who had time shares and airline miles which helped defray expenses. Unexpected funds became available and other good fortune. Once people knew of my intentions, things started happening naturally and it all came together.

You can do the same! Remind yourself – it is your life and you can design it any way you would like!

Chapter Ten
Discussion Questions

1. If money and time were no object, daydream about the vacations you would take. Write a list. Pick one or two for this year and put it on your calendar. Figure out when, where, the budget, and possible ways to fund it.

2. Spend one to two minutes writing a list of fun activities that you enjoy or would like to try. Write as fast as you can without thinking about the practicality of each item. Include things from watching the sunrise/sunset, walking the dog, a late-night swim, coffee with a girlfriend, skydiving, hitting golf balls, to taking horseback riding lessons. Later you can edit and prioritize the list. Pick a few items to do this week and add them to your schedule. Make it happen!

3. Think about how you felt planning these vacations and mini-vacations? Was your mood lifted? Are you happier and more positive? (You are likely already feeling the benefits of having some downtime.)

4. What vacation and fun activity are you now COMMITTED to doing?

My Downtime Plan:

MIX UP YOUR DAY

e have all experienced this — a very long, difficult day that was not necessarily productive. We need to make the best use of our day, not let the day make the best of us. One way is for YOU to run your day instead of it running you.

Performing high-focus work for hours on end is a sure way to burn out. It's better to tackle the more difficult work in chunks when you are at your peak operating mode.

For some people that is first thing in the morning. For someone else, it could be the afternoons.

These high-intensity tasks can be broken into "chunks" to accommodate breaks and stopping (or pausing) points, which helps with burn out.

Taking regular breaks instead of pushing through to completion are important. Just 5-10 minutes away from your desk helps to start again with more vigor. Sometimes you enter that zone where more time does not necessarily mean more productivity.

Often we tend to miss or delay our breaks and that can lead to poor performance. One such example for me, was trying to balance the checkbook late in the evening. I found it much better to put it aside until the morning.

Another way to take a break, but not in the usual sense of the word, is to tackle another sort of work that is easier to accomplish. Set a short time limit (10-20 minutes) so you don't eat up all your "good productivity" time. You are still working, but not taxing your brain so intensely.

By having a list of "easy" tasks to do, you can take a short break of sorts. This includes mini-organizing tasks, such as entering new contacts in your address book, sending quick emails to arrange coffee/lunch meetings, or sending a short thank you note. These items can be a welcome break.

For those women who work in the office as well as out of the office, an option is having "Focus" days and "Out of the Office" days. The goal is to schedule all your meetings, appointments and errands on the same days.

Then plan on other days to stay in the office to tackle complicated matters, reading reports, paperwork and phone calls. I have tried this method and found it to be a big help with time management!

Tip: when scheduling your Out of the Office Days – avoid too tight of a schedule. You can always arrive early to your next appointment and spend a few minutes composing yourself and thinking about the upcoming meeting. If you have too much excess time, use it to return phone calls or check emails.

It is not so much that there is one best way; it's a matter of finding the method that works best for you and your business. Keep trying until you find a method that works with your work style.

Chapter Eleven
Discussion Questions

1. What is your peak performance time? How do you plan it into your work day?

2. What big project or overwhelming task do you currently have that you could "chunk" down to smaller pieces?

3. Have you ever reached the level of non-performance on a task? If so, what did you learn? Do you have ideas on what might work for you to avoid such a situation in the future?

4. What tasks could you put on your "easy tasks" lists to serve as a break from focused work?

5. Would "Focus" days and "Out of the Office" days work for you? What types of tasks would you do on each day?

My Plan to Mix Up the Day:

CHAPTER TWELVE
ELIMINATE CLUTTER

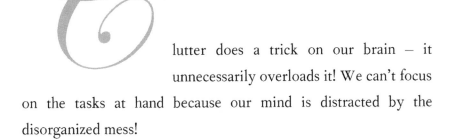

lutter does a trick on our brain — it unnecessarily overloads it! We can't focus on the tasks at hand because our mind is distracted by the disorganized mess!

We can solve that by creating a clean and organized work area. Start by setting up files with the appropriate information tucked neatly away (either virtually or physically), so your desk (and your mind) is clutter-free.

Then set up a tracking mechanism (like a calendar or to do list) so you can schedule WHEN to work on that item. Use technology to help manage your work and your time so you are more efficient.

Enlist the help of a professional organizer if the thought of de-cluttering or organizing your work space is overwhelming. These professionals can help you figure out systems that work for you, your work style, and your type of business.

Stop multi-tasking! You can work quicker and more efficiently if you do ONE thing at a time. Hone in on your focus skills. Concentrate on the work at hand, not the multitude of other items to be done.

Work at your pace. Do one thing and do it well. Avoid overscheduling as it can lead to stress and lack of focus while you are worried about the next upcoming thing.

A clean, organized work environment will aid tremendously in your productivity as well as your mind-set!

Chapter Twelve
Discussion Questions

1. Is your work space organized to be efficient and clutter-free? If not, what could you do to improve it?

2. When you have tried multi-tasking in the past, how did it go? What was the level or accuracy of your work?

3. When you tried focusing on one task at a time, at your own pace, how did that go?

My Plan to Eliminate Clutter:

CHAPTER THIRTEEN

BE "IN THE MOMENT"

ou can enjoy life more if you actually stop the distractions and turn your attention to the activity or event at hand.

You can do so if you turn off the technology and stifle your urges to check emails, phone messages, or Facebook constantly.

If you are at a luncheon, engage with the people next to you. Scan the room for people you know and want to reconnect.

Sometimes just a friendly face and short exchange will lift your day.

Maybe you've wanted to ask them something or perhaps your "welcoming look" may stir them to ask you something in your area of expertise.

Should you be with one person or just a couple friends, by all means, it's even more important to be "in the moment"! These people have set aside time from their busy schedule to be with you, so plan to be with them too. It is downright rude to text, check emails, or take phone calls if you are enjoying a meal with someone or at a meeting.

In the case of emergencies, you can explain ahead why you are checking your phone. If you really and truly have so many emergencies that attending an event is distracting, then consider just not attending. Perhaps it is the best choice for you and the other attendees.

We need to be in the moment to capture those meaningful moments of our lives! The emails, phone calls and posts can wait just a bit.

Chapter Thirteen
Discussion Questions

1. Have you been guilty of not being "in the moment"? Was it really necessary? If you are guilty of this behavior, what could you do to start to curtail it a bit?

2. Have you experienced being around someone who is constantly using their phone or other technology? How did it make you feel?

3. What sorts of emergencies would you find valid for someone not paying attention at a meeting or event?

4. Have you considered that just because everyone else is checking their phone, that it still might not be courteous to the speaker?

5. Have you considered what you are missing, when you are not present?

My Plan to "Be in The Moment:"

JANIE JURKOVICH

CHAPTER FOURTEEN
DELEGATE

 elegating a portion of the items on your "To Do List" can be invaluable. It will save you time to do the other things that only you can do; which could translate to making more money or having the luxury of a few minutes to yourself.

Another reason to delegate is there are tasks that someone else can do better and quicker, not to mention they actually like doing it! I am thinking about I.T. work or house cleaning, tasks I really don't enjoy. For you it could be keeping the books or yard work.

Your time and energy might well be spent doing other tasks and you will feel better for it!

Learning to delegate can be difficult for those of us who want to be in control or think only they can do a job properly. You can learn to let go of those thoughts with determination and willful thoughts. Your mindset is what needs to change.

Thinking about the big picture and how delegating will make your life better is very helpful.

I remember when I first thought about having a housekeeper. We lived overseas, and the other wives had all hired one, mostly because it was incredibly inexpensive. My thinking at the time was, "I don't want someone in my house. What if they do it wrong?"

One girlfriend was so picky - she insisted her housekeeper put the furniture polish on the rag instead of spraying the furniture directly. Admittedly, this might be a better practice, but it hadn't even occurred to me, so it made me think - how important is it? If the job gets done at an acceptable level, does it really matter if it is done "my way?"

The same thing goes with loading or unloading the dishwasher. Most of us have lamented that our spouse, children or roommates don't know how to perform the task. But does it really matter as long as the job is done to an acceptable level?

You don't get a better grade or more accolades if your house is cleaner than the neighbor's. All you really get is more stress!

On the work side, learning to delegate is a definite game changer! Once I hired an assistant to do the bookkeeping duties, my life was forever changed. I had so much more time to do the work I needed to do, that only I could perform. And luckily, she loved doing the books and was much better at it!

A side benefit of delegating is that it tends to make YOU want to be more productive. If you hire someone to do a specific task so it frees your time, then you feel more committed to making those sales calls or whatever your line of work may be.

Think you can't afford it? Think again. If you can charge $50 per hour for your line of work, and can pay someone else $15 per hour, you can make enough to cover their pay plus the required taxes and still come out ahead.

Over time, you can exponentially increase your income. You

can see how hiring others can increase the scope of your business significantly.

You need to look at the end result you want, not the many reasons it won't work.

Life is too short to spend it doing tasks you don't like. Figure out ways to delegate and make it happen. Your new life will be much improved!

Chapter Fourteen

Discussion Questions

1. What one task could you delegate right now that would be easy to incorporate into your daily life? How would you go about making this change?

2. If money was no object which tasks would you hire someone to do? Is there a way you could make it happen?

3. Think about the many things you do each day. Are you setting unrealistic standards on any of them? Could you lighten up a bit on some of them? Maybe they don't need to be delegated - just delayed or deleted.

My Plan to Delegate:

JANIE JURKOVICH

STRETCH YOUR COMFORT ZONE

There's a philosophy about how we're all in our little comfort zone – think of a circle and we're tucked safely inside. Then we meet a challenge in life and we have to punch out of the comfort zone to meet that challenge.

Hence our comfort zone expands. Eventually, we begin to feel more comfortable after meeting that challenge and life returns to a comfortable status.

Then another challenge meets us and we respond by punching out the other side of the comfort zone. Wow – it expands again. With this continued type of action, growth occurs.

Our new comfort zone is greatly expanded over what it was previously. Those earlier events make us stronger and more able to cope with future events.

The only way to get more "comfortable" is to continue to stretch. We need to regularly stretch our comfort zone if we are to grow to our full potential!

By this I mean not only the challenges that just seem to occur in our lives, but also seeking out more challenges, forcing ourselves to grow and expand.

For example, when I was writing the original blog posts (later this book), I had to set an artificial deadline of Thursday night to post my blog. I knew if I didn't force myself with a deadline, it would never get accomplished. There would always be a delay.

Once people knew there would be a new post Friday morning, they made comments about looking forward to it. Then I really knew I had to deliver! The confidence I gained helped me set similar deadlines in future writings.

LIVE THE LIFE YOU HAVE IMAGINED!

By setting more difficult goals versus just squeaking by, we can reach a much higher level of accomplishment.

The more you stretch, the more your confidence grows.

The more your confidence grows, the more you stretch.

It is a great cycle to be in!

Chapter Fifteen
Discussion Questions

1. Think of a time when you were forced to stretch your comfort zone. How did you feel at first when presented with this challenge? How did you feel once you had met the challenge?

2. Recall a challenge or goal you set for yourself that you met. How did you feel once you accomplished it?

3. Meeting challenges tends to increase our confidence. Do you regularly set your sights on something further once a challenge has been met? If not, what is holding you back?

My Plan to Stretch My Comfort Zone:

PERSEVERANCE

My dad used to say "If it was easy, everyone would do it." As I got older, I realized he was talking about perseverance.

Merriam Webster defines perseverance as "the quality that allows someone to continue trying to do something even though it is difficult."

According to Vocabulary.com, "Perseverance is not giving up.

It is persistence and tenacity, the effort required to do something and keep doing it till the end, even if it's hard." Dad was right - not everyone has what it takes to get the job done.

Perseverance can be more important than a college degree or experience when it comes to getting results. I would venture to say it is a measure of a person's character because truly when the going gets tough, the tough get going.

Don't be afraid to persevere. What you learn along the way is priceless. You will find you CAN do more than you ever thought possible. You will come up with more ideas than you ever imagined; find strength when you thought you had none left; and you will build confidence.

Those who persevere tend to make it.

Chapter Sixteen

Discussion Questions

1. Think about a time when you DID NOT persevere. What happened and how did you feel?

2. Now think about an event when you struggled, kept going and finally persevered. What did you have to go through? What did you accomplish and how did you feel once you got there?

3. When you compare the incidents when you persevered and when you did not - how does that frame how you think about future challenges?

My Plan to Persevere: *(Think about specific situations or goals that could be a challenge for you.)*

LISTEN TO MUSIC!

 istening to music can change your mood. It is very creative by nature.

When you listen to uplifting, happy music, it puts your mind in a new place. When you listen to popular music from your younger years, it tends to take you back in time. Listening to romantic music can change your mood too. Religious music helps folks get in the mood to open up to their religious teachings. Meditative music can calm you down and drown out the noise in your head from a busy day.

Music helps many people get their work done and it can be a wonderful way to enjoy your exercise routine. With such profound effects of music and the ease in which we can infuse music into our lives, we all need to help shape our day in the desired direction by searching out music that helps us live a better life.

Find something you like; something that makes you feel happy, upbeat or serene. That feeling will permeate through your day!

What you listen to will help you can create the type of day you deserve.

Chapter Seventeen
Discussion Questions

1. How do you use music in your typical day? What types of music do you listen to?

2. When could you ADD music to your life? What type would you choose?

3. What methods of music do you use? How could you CHANGE your method to better reflect your taste and the type of mood you want to create?

My Plan to Infuse Music into My Life:

LIVE THE LIFE YOU HAVE IMAGINED!

CHAPTER EIGHTEEN

EMBRACE CHANGE!

 hange - It's going to happen. The sooner you figure that out, the better.

Take a look at the world, your industry, your city, your family and your friends and determine what the reality is. Don't try to change that reality. Put your efforts into solutions that will work in your given situation.

Even within a family, things change. Children mature

(hopefully!) and move out, parents pass away and people retire.

We as human beings are in constant flux.

Another example could be an employee who cannot do his job properly despite repeated training. Eventually it becomes clear that either you will need to place him in a different position or show him the door.

The same goes for a competent employee, over time, she will need a more challenging or lucrative position. There again, change will take place.

Failure to recognize change and learn suitable ways to deal with it will lead to great frustration and unhappiness. It's the equivalent of hitting your head against the wall, repeatedly. Painful, very painful, indeed.

Chapter Eighteen
Discussion Questions

1. Give some examples of changes you've experienced in your life the last few years.

2. How did you handle one of those "changes?" How could you have handled it differently?

3. Have there been situations where you were more pro-active (or could have been) when dealing with changes?

My Plan for Dealing with Change:

JANIE JURKOVICH

IGNORE THE NAYSAYERS

ou know them. They are your friends and relatives with the negative attitudes.

They are the ones who have ten reasons why your idea won't work, is a bad idea and why you shouldn't even attempt it.

You must learn to tune them out or at least not let them burst your bubble and throw you off course! You can listen politely and decipher if any of their complaints have merit. If so, develop ways to mitigate those concerns (if you feel a need to do so).

Accomplished people don't wait until every conceivable potential problem is solved before paving the way. It is more likely they will start with a vision and adjust when necessary.

You are a target when you step out to do, change or invent something. It's much easier to poke holes in someone else's plan rather than come up with your own.

Have you noticed how the naysayers tend to stay on the sidelines? You might want to think about why.

Chapter Nineteen
Discussion Questions

1. Name a time when you wanted to try something new and were met with negative comments from a friend or relative who just wanted to help you. How did it make you feel. Did their remarks quell your desires?

2. Think about this - do you want the naysayers to direct your life? Do you feel their comments are necessarily helpful to you?

3. If your naysayer is typically a person in your inner circle, how will you deal with him or her in the future?

My Plan to Deal with Naysayers: *(Use specific examples of comments you expect and how you will handle them.)*

JANIE JURKOVICH

TAKE THE HIGH ROAD

ventually, we all encounter conflict somewhere along life's highway. We may feel we are treated terribly unfairly. We may even consider taking action against those who mistreat us.

Ripping out their eyeballs or at least a strong punch in the face may seem like a good idea at the time, however a better option is to "take the high road," and respond with kindness or indifference. At a minimum, remain civil.

Notice there was no mention of retaliation. Later you will be happy you did so!

Your actions will avoid any future guilt and remorse on your part for your "misbehavin' ways." You can keep your head high knowing you handled things professionally or personally in the best way possible.

It's not just staying out of trouble that's important. Super stressful situations play havoc with one's health. Learning to control your actions will keep your demeanor calm and your mind in a happier place.

One thing that helps me is to realize we don't know all the facets that go into the actions of another individual. Perhaps they are upset about something that has nothing to do with you and are just lashing out. Cut them and yourself a break.

In short time, you will have forgotten about the conflict if you act calmly instead of escalating the situation.

Chapter Twenty
Discussion Questions

1. When was the last time you had a conflict with someone? How important was that conflict a week later? A month? A year?

2. Think about a time when you had a serious conflict and the situation escalated due to your actions or the other person's. How did you feel about the situation later?

3. How could the situation have been handled better?

My Plan to Deal with Conflict and Take the High Road:
(Make a list of possible scenarios and write them out as "If 'x' happens, I will do 'y.')

CHANGE YOUR ATTITUDE

Z ig Ziglar once said, "Change your attitude, change your life." Is this ever true!

Have you ever met a millionaire with a bad attitude? Ever met an accomplished person with a negative attitude? I think not. There is something about being around a person with a positive attitude that attracts others.

Problems are solved much easier with a "can do" attitude,

versus playing the blame game and looking for scapegoats. If you don't already have a naturally positive attitude, consciously work on looking at life differently and change your attitude. Your life will greatly improve!

Not sure how to change your attitude? Try these strategies:

- Listen to soothing music.
- Read something uplifting.
- Call a "positive" friend.
- Read a book or listen to a webcast about improving one's attitude.
- Be grateful for the good things in your life. (We all have something.)
- Smile. In the mirror. Every day. Until it sticks.

Something that works for you today might not work tomorrow. Keep trying until your attitude has been adjusted.

Chapter Twenty-One
Discussion Questions

1. Evaluate whether or not you have a positive attitude. What would your close friends say about your attitude?
2. In what areas in your life could your attitude be improved?
3. What method would help you to improve your attitude?

My Plan to Improve My Attitude or Maintain a Positive Attitude:

JANIE JURKOVICH

CHAPTER TWENTY-TWO
GIVE GRATITUDE

ften in our hectic lives, we take for granted the many wonderful things we experience. Your outlook can be changed instantly if you spend a few minutes each day being grateful for the many people and things you enjoy in your life.

Maybe it's a special friend or family member. Maybe you are grateful for the roses in your garden or the happy face (or lick!) from your dog. Even the little things can put you in a happier mood.

Some people do this first thing in the morning; others do it when they go to sleep at night. It's even better to reflect and give gratitude BOTH times. You will begin and end each day with a renewed outlook if you spend time being grateful for your many blessings.

I whole-heartedly recommend each person spend time, regularly, to fit in some gratefulness-reflection on their blessings and express those thoughts. Some people use a "gratitude journal", which is very helpful for recording your gratitude. It's also extremely helpful when you find yourself down in the dumps.

Re-reading past entries will lift your mood back where it needs to be in order to live your best life.

Our goal should be to eventually give gratitude throughout the day, throughout our lives, so that it is just part of our being. What does this look like, you ask? It's a person who is joyous and happy and grateful for every person, every animal, every living creature in our magnificent world.

It is a person who "beams" with happiness and gratefulness, so much so that others can see her light!

Chapter Twenty-Two
Discussion Questions

1. List 5 things you are grateful for (big or small). Don't overthink this. Just write what comes to mind right away.

2. Did you notice any difference in your mood, attitude or feelings after identifying only 5 reasons to be grateful? Can you sense what a difference this could make in your life?

3. How can you fit in a little time each day to be more grateful? When, where and how long could you do this?

My Gratitude Plan: *(Write out specific ways you will live your life more gratefully.)*

CHAPTER TWENTY-THREE

LOOK FOR THE LESSON

hen the road of life takes you on an unwanted turn, try to think about what you can learn from the experience.

You may have a dramatic life-changing event (we've all had something) that really knocks you to your knees: death, divorce, serious medical condition, terrible accident or job loss.

First, figure out how to pick yourself up and manage the situation. Once the dust has settled and you're on your way to your new "normal," take some time to reflect.

Look for the lesson. Think about how this change will affect you and others.

It's likely there is a reason. Not an "excuse" type of reason, but something you were meant to learn from this occurrence. You might not be able to identify a reason at the time, but later on in life you will understand more.

One example in my life was when my maternal G'mother passed away. Her three daughters and all of us grandkids were devastated. But afterwards I realized that Grandpa was able to develop much deeper and meaningful relationships with all of his daughters and grandchildren in following years.

This would never have occurred if G'ma was around as all the 'girls' spent time in the kitchen cooking and gabbing with barely a "hello" to Grandpa. We all got to know him so much better than we ever would have due to the circumstances that occurred.

Once you realize that change occurs to help us learn and grow, that it is a take-away to remind yourself when the next unwanted turn comes your way, not only will it help you to survive, but you can thrive because next time you can avoid similar circumstances or at least know how to handle them better.

Realize this will eventually make you stronger.

Chapter Twenty-Three
Discussion Questions

1. Think of an unwanted turn your life has taken. When it occurred you were devastated, but how do you feel now?
2. Can you think of any "lessons" you learned from such an experience?

My Plan to Look for the Lesson:

RISE TO THE CHALLENGE

ost of us are not doing the best we can in terms of work or personal life. By nature, most humans are lazy creatures and aren't spurred to live a better life unless we either have to or experience a life-changing event that makes us take stock of things.

Remember YOU CAN DO IT. It just takes a positive attitude, determination, and some skill. Positive self-talk will help you gain confidence if you don't have it.

Keep telling yourself, "I CAN do it," "I WILL do it," and I WON'T QUIT!"

Write an affirmation, which is a little note to read aloud about what you will accomplish and your ability to do so.

Figure out what skills you need to conquer the challenge. Sign up for a class or ask for help in learning the needed skill. Becoming more competent in a skill or ability, helps raise your confidence too.

As you meet challenges, your confidence will build and the next time you have a challenge, you will have a little confidence in "reserves" to draw upon.

Each challenge conquered increases your confidence level. Eventually, you will be telling yourself, "I am FEARLESS. I can do anything I can set my mind to."

And you will!

Chapter Twenty-Four
Discussion Questions

1. Name a challenge you met. How did you feel once you accomplished this?

2. Have you ever tried positive self-talk or affirmations? If so, what was the result? If not, are you willing to try it?

3. What is stopping you from setting new challenges and moving forward? What can you do to change that?

My Plan to Meet New Challenges: (*Write specific words and phrases you'll use to encourage youself to meet new challenges.*)

CHAPTER TWENTY-FIVE

LAUGH

*L*aughing is so good for us! There is no easier way to improve your mood. You can do it quickly and it's mostly free. Share a joke with a friend, play a silly board game, watch a funny "YouTube" video, watch kid's cartoons, or go to an improv or comedy club.

Think about what other fun activities could put a little laughter in your life.

Laugh at yourself, share your calamities with friends and get a good laugh recalling your trials. (It also helps put things in perspective.) Note: it's ok to make fun of yourself but resist the temptation to poke fun at others.

A friend of mine who was once a comedian on a cruise ship shared with me the fact his former (second) wife was good for years of jokes. The marriage didn't last, but their funny experiences together were fodder for hours and hours of jokes which he shared until tears ran down my face from laughing so hard!

It releases endorphins making us feel better. It's a medically proven benefit that all of us have experienced. You will feel better, happier and more joyful.

Make a conscious effort to include more laughter in your life.

Chapter Twenty-Five
Discussion Questions

1. Do you have a "funny friend" who shares jokes or tells comical stories? How do you respond to being around them?

2. Think of a couple quick activities you could do for just 5 minutes a day that would make you laugh. How and when could you incorporate these activities into your life?

3. Do you have a joke in your pocket? One you could tell someone to lift their spirits (or yours)? Look or listen for a good one. Practice it and then share. (If you're desperate to find a good joke, look online or call Zappos. They have a Joke of the Day!)

My Plan to Add Laughter to My Life:

JANIE JURKOVICH

WEALTH – GO & GET IT!

ealth is not a dirty word despite what some people believe. There is enough monetary wealth for everyone. If someone has more wealth than someone else, they are not taking anything away from another.

People tend to have hang-ups around wealth, like feeling they don't really deserve it, or feeling guilty if they are more prosperous than others in their social circle.

Be willing to accept good fortunes as they come your way. Encourage others to aspire, desire and work towards any monetary goals they may have. Be joyful for others, never jealous. It doesn't serve either of you.

I'd like to share an example of limited "wealth thinking" from my own life. I used to be so frugal it was robbing me of the joy of spending money. I wasted so much time deciding if I really wanted to spend money on certain things. It was a chore to make such little decisions.

Once I let go of the fear of "not having enough," I could spend time focusing on the big picture of how to create wealth without working myself to death pinching pennies to excess.

The purpose of monetary wealth is to use it to enrich other areas of your life, relieve your worries; and give you peace of mind. Monetary wealth will not bring happiness in itself, but it helps to bring a wealth of opportunity for enjoyment in other areas of life.

Lastly, it is important to mention there are many types of wealth: family, friends, time, memories and adventures. Think about what kind of wealth you want in your life or perhaps how monetary wealth can help you attain another type of "wealth" important to you.

Chapter Twenty-Six
Discussion Questions

1. Do you have any guilt about monetary wealth? How can you re-frame your self-talk to relieve that guilt?
2. How would additional monies improve your life?
3. If money was no object, what would you do differently in your everyday life? (Dream a little here.)

My Plan to Think of Wealth as a Positive Force in My Life:

JANIE JURKOVICH

DELETE TV FROM YOUR LIFE

hat a waste of time! If you're focusing on your life and living the best, most purposeful life you can, you need to quit or limit the boob tube.

TV can suck the minutes, hours and days out of your life. How many mindless hours of junk TV does one person really need to watch to "wind down" after a day at work? Not five hours.

Think about this: how many books could you have read if you devoted that much time on a regular basis each month? How much better would you be at golf, tennis, or biking if you spent just a fraction of your TV time learning a new skill?

What if you spent that time taking a class in your chosen career field? Would that mean a promotion or increased income stream?

News and other "supposed" news shows are a drain on your brain too. Think about this: how much news do you really need a day? How many crimes do you need to hear about daily?

Think about how you feel after hearing about the wars, crimes, and disasters and other negative activities each day.

Do you feel regenerated, invigorated, ready for the day? I think not. I'd venture to say you feel down, sad, and sorry you watched TV instead of hitting the gym or going for a morning walk or something that would start your day off on the right foot.

Those of us who have already learned to delete TV have found life to be happier and more joyful. An added bonus is the extra time to participate in fun activies...a painting class, reading a novel or miniature golf with friends.

This doesn't mean you can never watch your favorite team play a ball game or a special TV series, but limit the time to special shows or events. Be mindful about the time you spend watching TV and the content you observe.

Life is a participatory event, not a spectator sport from your armchair!

Chapter Twenty-Seven
Discussion Questions

1. What are your favorite TV shows? Is there a pattern of junk, news, or channel surfing?
2. How many hours of TV do you typically watch each week? How much time does TV eat up in each day?
3. What activities could you be doing instead of watching TV?

My Plan to Delete or Reduce TV-Watching:

FIND AND FOLLOW
YOUR BLISS

W e all have our own special "bliss," the thing that we just love, makes us happy and we just can't live without. Some of us know what our bliss is. Others are still struggling to identify it.

To find true happiness and live the life you have imagined, you need to figure out what the thing or things are that give you supreme joy in life. It takes some introspection, thought and self-analysis to figure it out. Just keep asking yourself, "Does X bring me joy? Does X make me truly happy?" Eventually you will hit it.

Once you know what your bliss is, follow it and you will see your life transform. You will be happier in your daily life, in your interactions with others, and the way you feel will be greatly improved!

Some examples of things I really truly enjoy are sunrises and sunsets, working in my yard, swimming, preparing meals for others, time spent with close friends, traveling to new places, and writing in my journal. I had to learn to consciously spend time doing the things I enjoyed.

I had to be mindful of those activities that robbed me of my joy - household and work tasks I disliked or wasn't very good at, and negative people. Once I was mindful about what to omit and what to expand in my daily life (even those small things), my life became immensely more joyful, happy and blissful.

Your bliss is not the same as mine. We all need to follow our own bliss for a happy and meaningful life.

Chapter Twenty-Eight
Discussion Questions

1. What things, people or activities bring you joy?
2. What things, people or activities definitely DO NOT bring you joy, but that other people may like?
3. How can you consciously select/edit your activities to reach a more blissful life?

My Plan to Find and Follow My Bliss:

JANIE JURKOVICH

WORK ON SELF-DEVELOPMENT

orking on your self-development has the same kind of benefits as reading—it expands your mind. It gets you thinking about life in new ways. It helps to open your mind.

Listen to CDs and audios, read books and magazines that inspire and motive you and are easy to fit into your day! As a start: Jim Rohn's "The Art of Exceptional Living," Napoleon Hill's

"Think and Grow Rich" and Darren Hardy's "The Compound Effect."

Read the digital or print version of Success magazine for monthly inspiration from business leaders and entrepreneurs so that new ideas can be assessed and incorporated into your life. Learning helps you lead a better, more full-filled life. Listen to Ali Brown's audio interviews on Glambition Radio of women business owners.

There is a ton of information available on line, too. Find an author/coach/leader that inspires you and get in the habit of working on your self-development.

Ask your friends and business associates which business leaders they are following on social media. Find out what self-improvement books they are reading. Ask for suggestions. Make it a point to read/listen a minimum of 30 minutes a day. Your efforts will transform your life to a new level.

Don't have the time? Pop in a CD while you are driving or listen to a podcast when you're on the treadmill. Even the busiest people can do that.

Chapter Twenty-Nine
Discussion Questions

1. What would you like to learn to do better in your work life?
2. What would you like to learn to do better in your personal life?
3. How could you find out more about the above two topics? Make a list of possible actions you could take right away.

My Self-Development Plan:

JANIE JURKOVICH

REALIZE LIFE IS A JOURNEY

he biggest favor you can do for yourself as you work towards The Life You Have Imagined, is to realize as much effort as you put into improving your life and working towards your best life, you will never have it all together.

That doesn't mean don't try; it means give it your all and realize you still will be less than perfect. There will be setbacks. There will be disappointments.

There will be times when you want to throw up your hands and shout "what the hell!"

But don't give up. The journey is part of life's lesson. We learn to be tough. We learn to persevere. We learn how much we have gained by giving it our all.

Think about where you might be if you had not tried. It's probably quite a different outcome!

Chapter Thirty
Discussion Questions

1. What affirmation or self-talk can you write down now to refer to later, in time of stress and doubt, when you might consider giving up?

2. Write a list of reasons WHY it's important to you to live your best life, one where you are truly happy and fulfilled.

My Plan to Keep on Course Through the Journey of Life:

JANIE JURKOVICH

THE NECESSARY COMPONENTS

What are the components that are necessary for YOU to live the life you have imagined?

Take a look at your notes from the beginning of this excursion. Make some additions and changes if necessary. What kind of life did you imagine? Think about what needs to happen to get there.

Carry this book with you as a reminder to make it happen.

Or, if you are going to put this book back on the shelf, make a calendar appointment for three, six or twelve months from now to revisit your answers. It's hard to know how much you've grown and changed unless you are able to look at where you started.

It won't happen automatically...you must work on it. Be patient; it will take time. In fact, it most likely will take years to hone your behaviors to fit the life you have imagined.

That's the beauty of living the life you have imagined - you get to choose exactly how you want to live it!

Chapter Thirty-One
Discussion Questions

1. What have you learned by going through this process? Any newfound direction for your life? Are you ready to go off of "auto-pilot"?

2. Are you willing to do what it takes to make these changes? What is your motivation?

My Plan to Keep on Course Through the Journey of Life:

JANIE JURKOVICH

AFTERWORD

never imagined that after 35 years of marriage and devoting my life to the care of my children, my home, my spouse and my job, that I would find myself divorced, lost and wondering what happened.

I knew that I had to do something. What it was and how to do it was a complete mystery to me. I began to read, reflect and explore. As you might imagine, my ex-husband immediately began to ridicule me. I guess he never considered that someone could take on the massive task of completely revising their life. His snide comments only made me that much more determined to take charge of my own life and create the life I imagined.

You might be at such a crossroads in your life right now. Once you start making changes, not everyone is going to encourage you.

Not everyone will want you to change. You must ignore them! Find people who want you to succeed, who are supportive and who want you to live your best life. As I said in the dedication to this book, I am one of those people!

This book was written for you! You are not alone. You are not a failure. And your story is not written, no matter your age. As long as you have breath in your body, you can strive to live the life you have imagined.

I want to hear from you about your successes and your setbacks. Reach out to me at JanieJ@JanieJ.net

Here's to you and the life you have imagined living!

Janie J

WHAT TO DO NEXT

ongratulations on finishing "Live the Life You Have Imagined." Before you put it back on the shelf, put a reminder on your calendar for three, six and twelve months from now to review your progress.

Get Your Free Bonus

I've put all of the "Discussion Questions" together in one, easy-to-print downloadable document which you can use to write down and review your answers and plans. Go to www.JanieJ.net/bonus to get yours now.

Plus, you'll be among the first to know about my new books, journals and more!

JANIE JURKOVICH

ABOUT THE AUTHOR

anie Jurkovich spent 35 years of her life caring for her children, her spouse, her home, and her work.

When her marriage suddenly ended, she realized she had completely neglected to take care of herself. Despite successfully managing $6.6 million in properties as the owner of Jurkovich Doak Development, she was exhausted and truly lost. This was not the life she had imagined for herself at 25. Now, at 64, she is an author, a speaker, a competitive athlete, a business owner and a world traveler. This *IS* the life she imagined and it only gets better. She continues to engage in daily reflection, reading and exploration.

Discover more about her ongoing journey at www.JanieJ.net.

THE RACE

Standing at the gate
Waiting for the gun shot
She can barely wait
To run the race of her life.

Being held back by the bar
Only a few seconds more
And the life she is meant to live will start.

The thoroughbred will be let loose
To run around the track
So fast, so clear of her final destination.

I am the horse waiting for my journey to begin
On the racetrack of my life.
Let the race begin!

~ Janie Jurkovich

Attributions

Marketing consulting, interior design and editing by Beth Bridges, eBridge-Marketing.com

Logo and cover design by Ellie Dote, EllieGirlCreations.com

Author photo by Suzanne Moles, WattleWeb.com

Images by :
Chapter 1: Copyright elenanaum / 123RF.com Stock Photo
Chapter 2: Copyright cteconsulting / 123RF.com Stock Photo
Chapter 3: Copyright natashachetkova / 123RF.com Stock Photo
Chapter 4: Copyright setory / 123RF.com Stock Photo
Chapter 5: Copyright glopphy / 123RF.com Stock Photo
Chapter 6: Copyright moniqcca / 123RF.com Stock Photo
Chapter 7: Copyright yulianas / 123RF.com Stock Photo
Chapter 8: Copyright nathings / 123RF.com Stock Photo
Chapter 9: Copyright arkela / 123RF.com Stock Photo
Chapter 10: Copyright moniqcca / 123RF.com Stock Photo
Chapter 11: Copyright lenm / 123RF.com Stock Photo
Chapter 12: Copyright elvetica / 123RF.com Stock Photo
Chapter 13: Copyright mrcocoa / 123RF.com Stock Photo
Chapter 14: Copyright rastudio / 123RF.com Stock Photo
Chapter 15: Copyright jjesadaphorn / 123RF.com Stock Photo
Chapter 16: Copyright jjesadaphorn / 123RF.com Stock Photo
Chapter 17: Copyright oxygen64 / 123RF.com Stock Photo
Chapter 18: Copyright moniqcca / 123RF.com Stock Photo
Chapter 19: Copyright bersonne / 123RF.com Stock Photo
Chapter 20: Copyright retrorocket / 123RF.com Stock Photo
Chapter 21: Copyright gomolach / 123RF.com Stock Photo
Chapter 22: Copyright zhenyakot / 123RF.com Stock Photo
Chapter 23: Copyright robuart / 123RF.com Stock Photo
Chapter 24: Copyright aurielaki / 123RF.com Stock Photo
Chapter 25: Copyright artinspiring / 123RF.com Stock Photo
Chapter 26: Copyright tsirik / 123RF.com Stock Photo
Chapter 27: Copyright yupiramos / 123RF.com Stock Photo